# I am a
# MUSLIM

# I am a
# MUSLIM

**Manju Aggarwal**
meets
**Abu Bakar Nazir**

## Photography: Chris Fairclough

Religious Consultant:
Sheikh Jamal M. A. Solaiman

## FRANKLIN WATTS
LONDON/NEW YORK/SYDNEY/TORONTO

Abu Bakar Nazir is eleven years old. He and his family are Muslims. His father, Mohammed Nazir, is a bus driver in Birmingham, England. His mother, Zarina Nazir, is a housewife. Abu's eldest sister, Maria, is nine. He has three other sisters: Sarah, who is seven, Ayshah, who is six, and Hafsah, who is three.

# Contents

© 1985 Franklin Watts Ltd

First published in the USA by
Franklin Watts Inc.
387 Park Avenue South
New York
N.Y. 10016
US ISBN: 0-531-10020-0
Library of Congress Catalog
  Card Number: 85-50168
Printed in Hong Kong

The Publishers would like to
thank the Nazir family and
all other people shown in
this book. Special thanks
are also due to James
Pailing for his help and
encouragement in the
preparation of this book.

Manju Aggarwal is Co-
ordinator for South Asian
Languages for the London
Borough of Newham.

Sheikh Jamal M. A.
Solaiman is Imam of the
Central Mosque, Regents
Park, London.

# The Muslim belief

My family are Muslims. We follow a religion called Islam which began in Arabia when the Prophet Muhammad first heard the word of God.

Muhammad was born in Mecca in 570 A.D. At that time the Arabs had many beliefs and gods. When Muhammad was about forty he felt himself called to become a Prophet of God's Message. He taught that there is only one God—as believed by Jews and Christians. The rest of his life was spent revealing God's Message. God is called Allah in Arabic.

**We believe that God's Message as revealed to Muhammad is found in the Koran, our Holy Book.**

The most important Message of the Koran is that God is the creator of the world and controls everything in it. Muslims are called upon to surrender to the will of God. In Arabic, Muslim means "one who gives himself to God." Islam means "submission or obedience to God." Muslims must live according to rules found in the Koran.

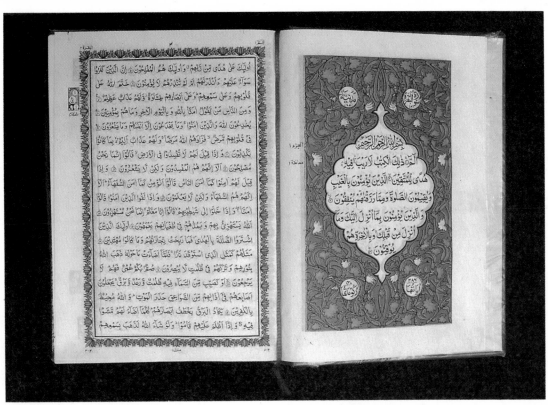

## Muslim Law

**As a Muslim I have five main duties to perform—the Five Pillars of Islam.**

The first duty is shahada (affirmation). The muslim declares his faith by saying: "There is no god but God, and Muhammad is His Messenger." The second is salat (prayer). Prayers must be said five times a day. The third is zakat (almsgiving). A Muslim must give money to good causes. The fourth is siyam (fasting). In the month of Ramadan healthy Muslims must not eat or drink from dawn to dusk. The last duty is to make a pilgrimage (hajj) to the holy city of Mecca.

**I have to follow many other rules to become a good Muslim.**

Islam gives guidance on all aspects of life. Muslims cannot eat pork and other meats must be prepared in a way called halal. They should not drink alcohol. They should not fight except for Islam. They must not gamble. Muslims should not be stingy and must be kind to strangers. Great numbers of books have been written on the teachings of Muhammad and the laws of Islam.

## Going to the Mosque

**At midday on Friday I go with my family to the Mosque to worship with other Muslims.**

A Muslim place of worship is called a Mosque. A Mosque usually has a dome and a tower called a minaret. A man called a Muezzin stands at the top of the minaret and calls Muslims to prayer. Mosques are built so that the people face Mecca when they pray. The Mosque is the center for many Muslim activities.

## We must remove our shoes and wash ourselves in a special way.

Muslims enter the Mosque in bare feet as a mark of respect to God. They also have to make sure that they are in a pure state by doing a ceremony called Al-wudhu. This begins by speaking the name of God. Then the hands are washed, followed by the mouth, the nostrils and face. Next the arms are washed from wrist to elbow, the right arm first, before the head and ears. Last, both feet are washed up to the ankles.

# Inside the Mosque

We use prayer mats in the Mosque. When we pray the mat must face Mecca.

The main halls of Mosques are just open spaces. There is an alcove called the Mihrab which shows the direction of Mecca. There is also a pulpit for the preacher. No pictures of any living things are allowed in a Mosque. This is so that the faithful will think only of God.

**Prayers in the Mosque are led by the Imam. We have a sermon on Fridays.**

There are no special ceremonies or services in a Mosque such as are found in Christian churches. The prayers said in the Mosque are the same as those said anywhere else. The prayers last for about ten minutes. Women are not allowed to pray with men. They worship in a different part of the Mosque.

## Muslims at prayer

**I must say my prayers five times every day. All prayers are said in Arabic.**

Prayers are said in the early morning, early afternoon, late afternoon, sunset and at night. At home, as in the Mosque, shoes are taken off and the washing is done before praying. Prayers are said in Arabic as it is the language of the Koran.

14

The prayer begins in the standing position to show that one is listening to God and wants God to hear the prayer. The opening verses of the Koran are said—"God is great." The Muslim then bows to show respect to God. Then the ground is touched with the forehead, knees, nose and palms of the hands. This is done twice. At the end of the prayer one kneels to pray for Muhammad and all Muslims. Then one turns the head to the right and left saying "Peace be on you and God's blessings."

# The History of Abu's family

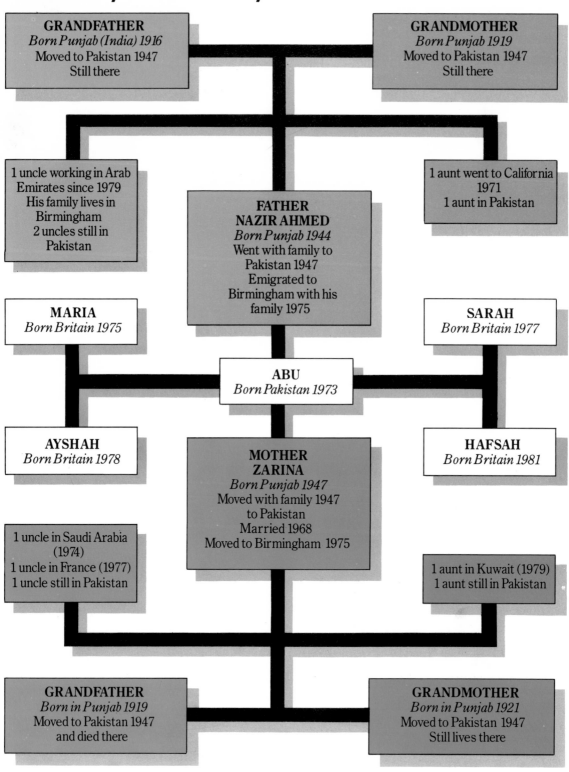

**GRANDFATHER**
*Born Punjab (India) 1916*
Moved to Pakistan 1947
Still there

**GRANDMOTHER**
*Born Punjab 1919*
Moved to Pakistan 1947
Still there

1 uncle working in Arab
Emirates since 1979
His family lives in
Birmingham
2 uncles still in
Pakistan

**FATHER
NAZIR AHMED**
*Born Punjab 1944*
Went with family to
Pakistan 1947
Emigrated to
Birmingham with his
family 1975

1 aunt went to California
1971
1 aunt in Pakistan

**MARIA**
*Born Britain 1975*

**SARAH**
*Born Britain 1977*

**ABU**
*Born Pakistan 1973*

**AYSHAH**
*Born Britain 1978*

**HAFSAH**
*Born Britain 1981*

**MOTHER
ZARINA**
*Born Punjab 1947*
Moved with family 1947
to Pakistan
Married 1968
Moved to Birmingham 1975

1 uncle in Saudi Arabia
(1974)
1 uncle in France (1977)
1 uncle still in Pakistan

1 aunt in Kuwait (1979)
1 aunt still in Pakistan

**GRANDFATHER**
*Born in Punjab 1919*
Moved to Pakistan 1947
and died there

**GRANDMOTHER**
*Born in Punjab 1921*
Moved to Pakistan 1947
Still lives there

## The Koran

**The Koran, our Holy Book, is always treated with great respect. We must not let it touch the ground or get dirty.**

When not in use the Koran is kept wrapped in cloth. Muslims believe that the Koran is the word of God himself. They do not believe that Muhammad wrote it. They say that he memorized it as it was revealed to him by the angel Gabriel and recited it to his followers. Koran in arabic means recitation. It was put in written form before Muhammad's death. Passages from the Koran are often beautifully decorated.

**I have to learn the Koran by heart and recite it in the proper way.**

A Muslim who can recite the Koran from memory is called a Hafiz. It is thought to be a sign of great excellence. The Koran has 114 chapters or suras. It must be read in Arabic. It is believed that it will not be the word of God in any other language. Every Mosque has a Koran school. Muslims should also read books called the Hadith which tell what Muhammad did and taught.

Arabic Script

| | | |
|---|---|---|
| Q ق | Z ز | A ا |
| K ك | S س | B ب |
| L ل | SH ش | T ت |
| M م | S ص | TH, Ṭ ث |
| N ن | Ḍ, Z ض | J ج |
| W, V و | T ط | H ح |
| H ه | Z ظ | KH خ |
| ٴ | AI ع | D د |
| Y يى | GH, G غ | Z ذ |
| | F ف | R ر |

## Muslim Clothes

**I went with my mother and sister to buy material for my sister's new suit.**

There is no special dress in Islam, but the Koran tells Muslims to cover their bodies. A man must cover his body from the waist to the knee, and a woman should cover herself from the head to the feet except for her hands and face. Apart from these rules Muslims can wear the normal clothes of the country in which they live.

## When we go to the Mosque we prefer to wear Pakistani clothes.

Most of the Muslims in Britain came from Pakistan and Bangladesh. Many women and some men can be seen wearing the traditional Pakistani and Bangladeshi clothing called the salwar kameez. These are loose trousers drawn in tightly at the ankles, with a loose shirt. When Muslim men pray they cover their heads as a mark of respect to God.

## Eating the Muslim way

**We can only eat certain meats and we must go to a special butcher for them.**

Muslims are forbidden to eat meat from the pig or any food cooked in pork fat. Lamb and beef can be eaten provided the animal has been killed in a special way. Meat prepared in the Muslim way is called halal, meaning "allowed." All other foods can be eaten. Muslims are forbidden to drink alcohol as it can make a person lose self-respect and become an object of shame.

I wash my hands and rinse my mouth before and after each meal. I also say my prayers before the meal and thank God afterwards.

All Muslims wash and say prayers before and after a meal. The eldest person in the family starts eating first unless there are guests. The guests always begin first. Abu's family eats Pakistani foods such as curried meats, kebabs and rice.

## Pilgrimages to Mecca

**Last year I went with my father to Mecca to do the Umra, the lesser pilgrimage. I had to wear the clothes of the pilgrim.**

Mecca is the most holy city of Islam. In the Umra the pilgrim follows a traditional route and does special ceremonies at the holy places. The Umra can be made at any time of the year. The Hajj, the chief pilgrimage, can only be made in the month of Dhul Hijjah.

Every year about two million Muslims make the Hajj. The central place for worship is the courtyard of the Great Mosque. In the middle is the Ka'ba, a small stone building containing the Black Stone. Muslims believe that this was given to Abraham by God 4,000 years ago. During the Hajj pilgrims walk around the Ka'ba seven times and try to kiss the Black Stone. On the eighth day of the month pilgrims travel from Mecca to Mina. They then go on to Arafat and back to Mina by the morning of the tenth day.

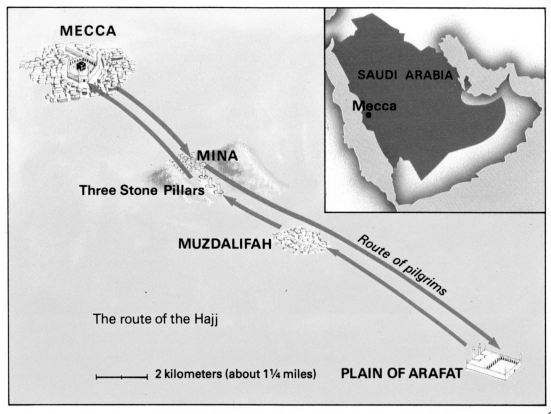

MECCA

SAUDI ARABIA

Mecca

MINA

Three Stone Pillars

MUZDALIFAH

Route of pilgrims

The route of the Hajj

2 kilometers (about 1¼ miles)

PLAIN OF ARAFAT

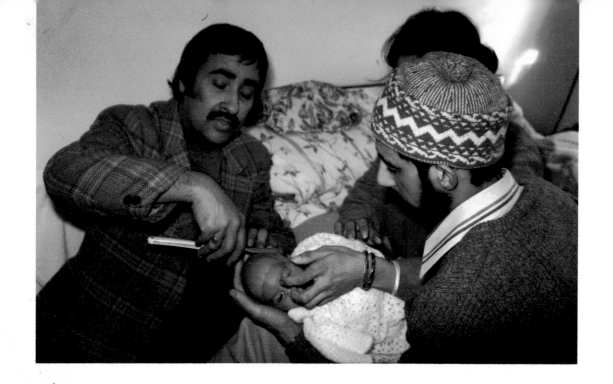

## Muslim customs

**When I was a tiny baby my head was shaved and prayers were recited over me.**

All children of Muslim parents are at once brought into the faith. The father must teach his children the Muslim religion. Children must obey their parents in all things even when they are grown up. Marriages are usually arranged by parents. A girl may be married to someone she has not met before. In special cases a Muslim man may have more than one wife but this is not common now.

**I look forward to weddings. Beautiful clothes are worn and there is a party.**

The man proposes marriage and the woman agrees in front of two witnesses. The Qadi (judge) then says how much dowry (money) the bridegroom is to give to his bride. The marriage is then blessed by a reading from the Koran. Candy is then given to the guests. The bridegroom then takes the bride home. The next day there is a party called a Walima. The bridegroom wears a special headdress.

# The Muslim Year

The Muslim months of the year begin with each new moon. This means that the Muslim year is ten days shorter than the western year. This means that the festivals are held during all seasons of the year.

The circular calendar shows the following Western months (outer ring): DECEMBER, RABI-UL, NOVEMBER, SAFAR, OCTOBER, MUHARRAM, SEPTEMBER, DHUL-HIJJAH, AUGUST, DHUL-QAADAH, JULY, SHAWWAL, RAMADAN (with Muslim months on the inner ring).

## MEELAD-UL-NABI
### (BIRTHDAY OF THE PROPHET MUHAMMAD)
*Rabi-Ul-Awwal – 1 day*
The 12th day of the 3rd month when the message of the Koran was given to believers through Muhammad.

## MUHARRAM (NEW YEAR)
*Muharram – 1 day*
Umar, 2nd Caliph, fixed this as the 1st month of the year. It also commemorates the Hegira, Muhammad's departure from Mecca to Medina in AD622.

## EID-UL-ADHA
### (FEAST OF SACRIFICE)
*Dhul-Hijjah – 1 day*
The high point of the Hajj. At Mina, where Abraham showed his willingness to sacrifice Ishmael, a sheep is sacrificed. For those who visit the Holy Places at different times to the Hajj, a feast known as Umra is held.

## EID-UL-FITR
*Shawwal – 1 day*
The first day of the new moon and the end of Ramadan. A joyful feast when new clothes are worn and presents exchanged.

## RAMADAN
*Ramadan – 1 lunar month*
A month of fasting, when the Muslim does not eat between dawn and dusk. It is observed as one of the 5 pillars and is the only month referred to in the Koran.

## LAILAT-UL-QADR
*Ramadan – 1 night*
The night of the 26th day of Ramadan. Known as 'the night of power' when Muhammad received the first revelation from the Angel Gabriel.

Around the circular calendar edge (months):

JANUARY · FEBRUARY · MARCH · APRIL · MAY · JUNE

WWAL · RABI-UL-AKHIR · JAMADI-UL-AWWAL · JAMADI-UL-AKHIR · RAJAB · SHA'BAN

**LAILAT-UL-ISM WAL MI'RAJ**

*Rajab – 1 night*

The night of the journey and the Ascension. Celebrated on the 26th Rajab, this marks the Prophet's night journey from the Ka'ba in Mecca to the rock in Jerusalem.

**LAILA-UL-BARH**

*Sha'ban – 1 night*

The night of forgiveness, a fortnight before the start of Ramadan.

# Muslim facts and figures

Islam is the second largest religion in the world with about 600 million followers. Christianity is the largest with about 1,000 million.

The countries in which over 90 per cent of the population are Muslim include Afghanistan, Algeria, Egypt, Indonesia, Iran, Iraq, Morocco, Pakistan, Turkey and Saudi Arabia.

The country with the largest Muslim population is Indonesia with over 100 million followers. The next is Pakistan with around 80 million, followed by India and Bangladesh.

In the U.S. there are about two million Muslims. The majority come from Syria, Lebanon, Iran, India, and Turkey. Some have come from Russia and Poland.

The history of Islam begins in 622 AD with the flight of Muhammad (the Hegira) from Mecca to Medina. He then started the Islamic community which was to rule almost all of Arabia by his death in 632 AD.

By 750 AD Muslim armies had built a huge empire including North Africa, Spain, Palestine, Syria, Persia, Iraq and parts of India. For many centuries there was a great Muslim civilization from which Europe learned much, especially in science and medicine.

Many Muslim beliefs are similar to those of Jews and Christians. They believe, for example, that there is heaven and hell after death. Abraham and Moses of the Old Testament and Jesus Christ are respected as great prophets by Muslims. Muhammad is said to be the last and greatest prophet.

The place of Muslim women until recently was always thought to be in the home. If they went outside a veil had to be worn. This view is changing in most Muslim countries.

Islam allows a man to have up to four wives in certain cases. It is now rare to have more than one and is forbidden in some Muslim countries.

The largest Mosque in use today is the Umayyad Mosque in Damascus, Syria. The tallest minaret is at the Sultan Hassan Mosque in Cairo, Egypt.

# Glossary

**Allah** The Muslim name for God.

**Arabic** The language of the Arabs.

**Hadith** Books which tell what Muhammad did and taught.

**Hajj** The Muslim pilgrimage to the Ka'ba at Mecca in Saudi Arabia during the month of Dhul Hijjah.

**Halal** Arabic word for allowed.

**Imam** One who leads Muslims in prayer in the Mosque.

**Islam** The Muslim religion. The word in Arabic means submission or obedience.

**Koran** The Muslim holy book, believed to be the actual words of God revealed to Muhammad.

**Ka'ba** The building in Mecca housing the Black Stone which is the center of Muslim prayer.

**Mecca** The Muslim holy city in Saudi Arabia.

**Minaret** The tower on a Mosque from which Muslims are called to prayer.

**Mosque** The Muslim place of worship.

**Muhammad** The founder of the religion of Islam.

**Muslim** One who submits himself to God by following the religion of Islam.

**Ramadan** The ninth month of the Muslim year. Muslims must fast from dawn to dusk during Ramadan.

**Salat** Muslim prayer: one of the Five Pillars of Islam.

**Shahada** Public affirmation of faith in God. One of the Five Pillars of Islam.

**Siyam** Fasting as done in the month of Ramadan. One of the Five Pillars of Islam.

**Umra** The lesser Pilgrimage to Mecca.

**Zakat** The giving of alms (gifts) to good causes—the poor or Mosques. One of the Five Pillars of Islam.

# Index